I Am A Dinosaur

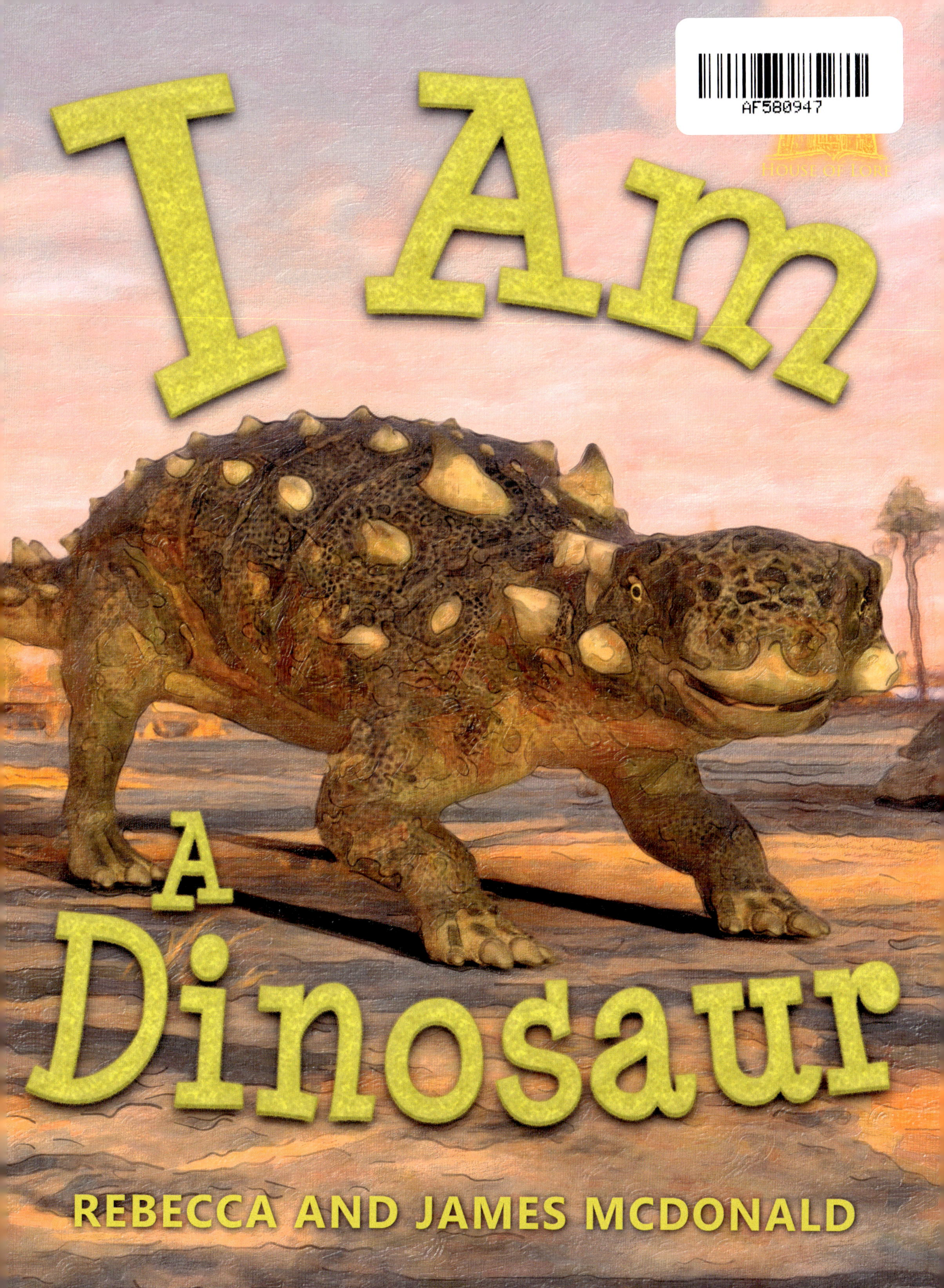

REBECCA AND JAMES MCDONALD

Ang-kyle-uh-sore-us

I am a dinosaur. I roamed the Earth millions of years ago. My name is **Ankylosaurus.** I have tough armor and sharp spikes on the top side of my body. My tail has a thick round bone on the end that I can swing like a hammer.

My favorite foods are leaves and shrubs. Scientists call creatures that only eat plants herbivores. Many dinosaurs were herbivores. Scientists who study dinosaurs are called Paleontologists.

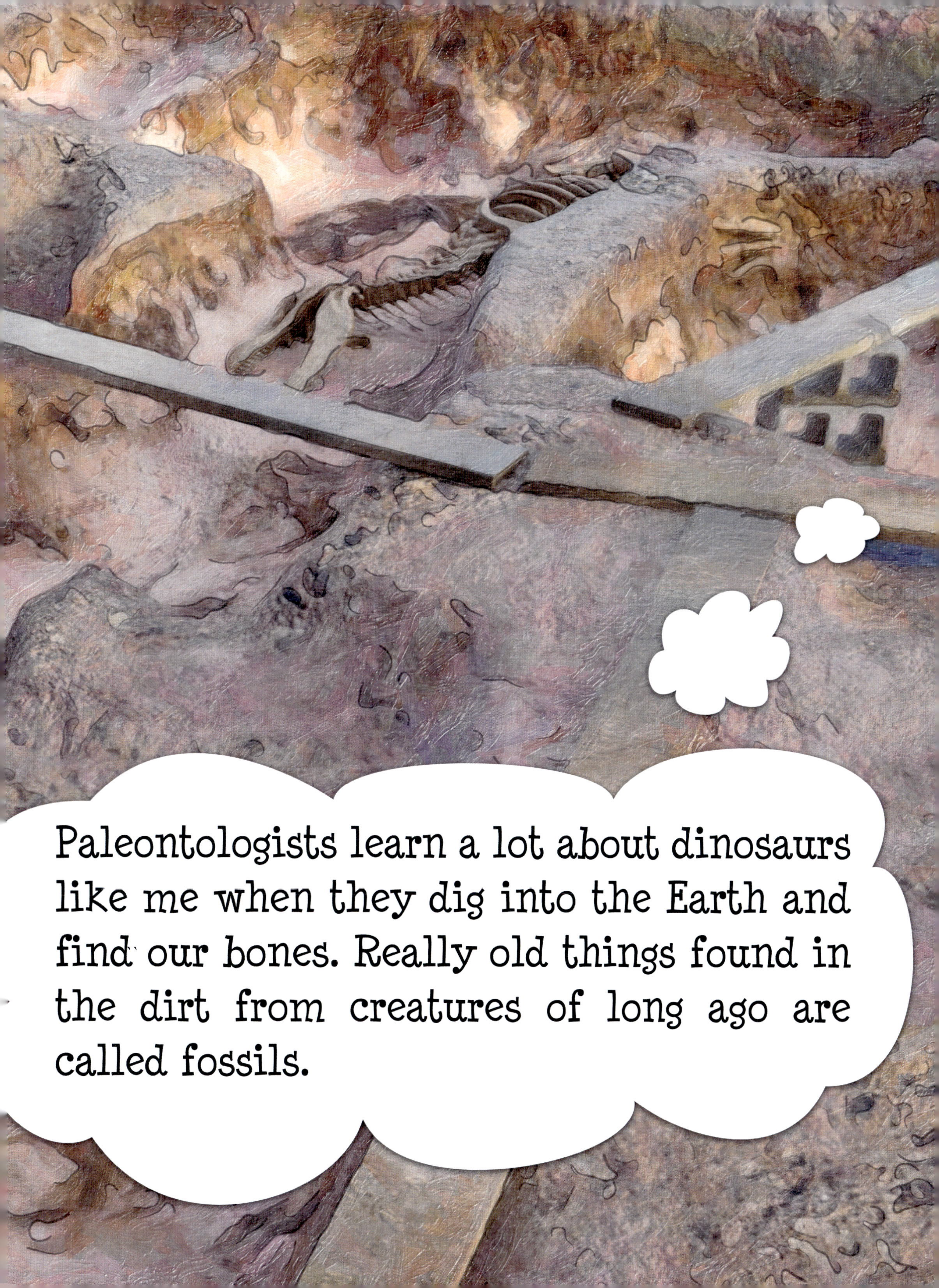
Paleontologists learn a lot about dinosaurs like me when they dig into the Earth and find our bones. Really old things found in the dirt from creatures of long ago are called fossils.

Paleontologists have also found fossils of dinosaurs that liked to eat other dinosaurs. Creatures that like to eat meat are called carnivores. Dinosaur fossils have been discovered all over the world. Let's meet a few.

My name is Alamosaurus. I'm an herbivore. I have spikes and armor up and down my back to protect myself.
Al-um-oh-sore-us

My name is **Spinosaurus.** I am the biggest carnivore of all. I have sharp teeth and claws for hunting. I spend a lot of time in rivers, poking my long snout out of the water like a crocodile.
Spine-uh-sore-us

Steg-oh-sore-us

My name is **Stegosaurus.** I'm an herbivore. I have plates on my back and a spiked tail for defending myself. Scientists say I have a really small brain, but I'm smart enough to know to use my spiked tail against dinosaurs trying to eat me.

My name is **Saurolophus**. I'm an herbivore. I can stand on my two back legs to reach tall plants, or I can stand on all four of my legs to search the ground for tasty twigs. I'm also a duck-billed dinosaur.
Sore-oh-loh-fus

My name is **Gallimimus.** I'm an omnivore. That means that I eat plants, meat, eggs and sometimes a juicy bug or two. I also like to run in packs with other dinosaurs just like me.

Gal-uh-my-mus

My name is **Brachiosaurus.** I'm an herbivore. I have a really long neck that helps me reach delicious leaves at the top of tall trees. My teeth are spoon-shaped, so I can scoop up lots of vegetation.

Dak-oh-tuh-rap-tor

My name is **Dakotaraptor.** I'm a carnivore, and the largest raptor-type of dinosaur that scientists have found. I'm unusual because I have long wings, but I can't fly. Sharp claws at the end of my wings and on my feet make me a really good hunter.

My name is **Pteranodon.** I am a dinosaur that can fly! I'm also a carnivore. When scientists found my fossils, they also found fish bones in my stomach.

Tur-an-oh-don

My name is **Styracosaurus**. I'm an herbivore. My mouth is shaped like a beak, so it's good for breaking and tearing vegetation that's tough as wood.

Sty-rack-oh-sore-us

My name is **Allosaurus**. I'm a carnivore. I stand on two strong legs and balance myself with a long tail. I lay eggs and then bury them for safety. When it's time for my eggs to hatch, I carefully dig them up.

My name is **Triceratops.** I'm an herbivore. The boney armor around my neck is called a frill. I also have two sharp horns above my eyes and a shorter horn on my nose. My armor and horns protect me from other dinosaurs that bite.

Dye-non-ick-us

My name is **Deinonychus**. I'm a carnivore, but I'm not a very big one. I have a large claw on each of my feet and long arms with claws that can grasp creatures that I want to eat.

My name is **Tyrannosaurus rex.** I'm a carnivore. Scientists think I'm one of the biggest carnivorous dinosaurs that ever lived. I have a giant mouth with super sharp teeth, great for tearing and eating lots of meat.

Tye-ran-uh-sore-us

Many scientists believe dinosaurs that stood on two legs like Tyrannosaurus rex, Deinonychus, and Gallimimus slowly grew into the feathered birds that live in our world today.

When you notice a bird flying in the sky or sitting on a branch in a tree, it's a little like seeing a miniature feathered dinosaur. It's amazing to think that the birds of today are relatives of the giant dinosaurs of long ago that rattled and shook the ground, searching the land for food.

Scientists aren't sure exactly how all of the dinosaurs died, but they have some good ideas like disease, a changing climate, lack of food, and possibly even a large object from outer space that struck the Earth, sending up clouds of dust that blocked the Sun and made it too cold.

People can see fossils and even some giant dinosaur skeletons on display at Museums of Natural History. Paleontologists are still finding and digging up new fossils. Who knows what they'll discover next!

What's your favorite dinosaur?

Can you find things about the herbivores that are similar?

What about the carnivores?

Are there any birds today that remind you of a dinosaur?

Why do you think some dinosaurs moved in packs?

Why would some dinosaurs bury their eggs?

I Am A Dinosaur

ISBN: 978-0-9982949-9-5
First House of Lore paperback edition, 2019
Visit us at www.HouseOfLore.net

I Am Earth
Rebecca and James McDonald
I Am the Solar System
REBECCA AND JAMES MCDONALD
I Am the Moon
REBECCA AND JAMES MCDONALD
I Am the Sun
REBECCA AND JAMES MCDONALD
I Am Spring
I Am A Bee
I Am A Frog
I Am A Dinosaur
CHECK OUT THESE OTHER TITLES FROM HOUSE OF LORE
I Am the Alphabet
REBECCA AND JAMES MCDONALD
Planting ABC in a Garden of Memory
Rebecca and James McDonald
ALPHA THE ALPHA-BOT
GUARDIAN OF THE ALFURBETS
THE ALPHABET BY COCKROACHES
REBECCA AND JAMES MCDONALD
The Scribbles
REBECCA AND JAMES MCDONALD
Rainy Day Poems
If You Don't Understand, Raise Your Hand
Bo the Bear BUILDS a Monster Truck
REBECCA AND JAMES MCDONALD
Wilford and Blue
The Kite Calamity
REBECCA AND JAMES MCDONALD
Wilford and Blue
Mud Madness
REBECCA AND JAMES MCDONALD
Why Mama Why

Made in the USA
Monee, IL
03 January 2024

51114376R00029